HUGS
From
HEAVEN

HUGS
From
HEAVEN

Walks *on the* Beach *with* Brian

Janice L. Avery St.Cyr

XULON ELITE

Xulon Press Elite
555 Winderley Pl, Suite 225
Maitland, Fl 32751
407.339.4217
Www.xulonpress.com

© 2024 By Janice L. Avery St.cyr

All Rights Reserved Solely By The Author. The Author Guarantees All Contents Are Original And Do Not Infringe Upon The Legal Rights Of Any Other Person Or Work. No Part Of This Book May Be Reproduced In Any Form Without The Permission Of The Author.

Due To The Changing Nature Of The Internet, If There Are Any Web Addresses, Links, Or Urls Included In This Manuscript, These May Have Been Altered And May No Longer Be Accessible. The Views And Opinions Shared In This Book Belong Solely To The Author And Do Not Necessarily Reflect Those Of The Publisher. The Publisher Therefore Disclaims Responsibility For The Views Or Opinions Expressed Within The Work.

Unless Otherwise Indicated, Scripture Quotations Taken From The New American Standard Bible (Nasb). Copyright © 1960, 1962, 1963, 1968, 1971, 1972, 1973, 1975, 1977, 1995 By The Lockman Foundation. Used By Permission. All Rights Reserved.

Paperback Isbn-13: 979-8-86850-514-0
Hard Cover Isbn-13: 979-8-86850-515-7
Ebook Isbn-13: 979-8-86850-516-4

Introduction

Human language speaks, communicates, addresses, and directs. It can be creative, descriptive, intellectual and spiritual. It can move the spirit to tears. It can bare a soul. Words never sound as deeply as they are felt. Words alone cannot always speak what the spirit is trying to say. Words of mourning are a minute expression imparting a fraction of a tiny fraction of the sorrow within the heart of someone feeling the loss of their loved one. Human tears, however, are a direct expression of the soul. A face can say what a heart feels. The only one who truly understands each of our hearts is Jesus, who is closer than the air we breathe, because His loving presence is within us. He knows every tear. He saves them in a bottle:

"Thou hast taken account of my wanderings; put my tears in Thy bottle." — Ps. 56:8

"O Lord, Thou hast searched me and known me. Thou dost know when I sit down and when I rise up; Thou dost understand my thought from afar…How precious also are Thy thoughts to me, O God! How vast is the sum of them! … Search me, O God, and know my heart; Try me and know my anxious thoughts; And see if there be any

hurtful way in me, And lead me in the everlasting way."
— Ps. 139:1-2, 17, 23-24

I wrote these words for my son. They are a simple expression of my overwhelming sorrow and the deepest part of my soul's pain. If my soul was my body, it was ripped in half when he died. If you are going through this pain, you will understand the words and they may reach the deepest part of your soul, too. I believe that life's greatest treasure is a child. Although some thoughts may sound extravagant, each word utters truth unimaginable. The pain is real. Wherever you see "Oh, my baby," or "Oh, my Brian," those are not just words. Those are pangs of mourning verbalized, a tormented heart vocalized. In the beginning, the pain is absolute torture. There are positively no words on earth that can describe this overwhelming feeling of loss and lostness, devastation, and pure tragedy. In this book of letters, I often refer to a *river of sadness* because that is what filled in the two halves of my heart. I became determined not to let sorrow overcome me and take over; otherwise, I would not have been able to survive. I learned to let sorrow reside in the same heart with joy, which I received in abundance from God, my family, and my friends.

The wound is always there, but the pain subsides, the longer time passes. Three years after Brian died, I noticed a remarkable difference in the intensity of my pain. Ten years have passed and I am much stronger now. Time heals but it does not cure. Only Jesus can do that. Pour out your hearts and keep on trusting:

"Trust in Him at all times, O people; Pour out your heart before Him; God is a refuge for us." — Ps. 62:8

God saved me: "Why are you in despair, O my soul? And why have you become disturbed within me? Hope in God, for I shall again praise Him for the help of His presence." —Ps. 42:5

He has been my counselor and my guide:

"…With Thy counsel Thou wilt guide me, and afterward receive me to glory." — Ps. 73:24

He is my strength, my joy, and my salvation:

"Behold, the Lord is my salvation. I will trust and not be afraid; for the Lord God is my strength and my song, and He has become my salvation." — Isa. 12:2

His presence within me comforts me every day. I did not understand why this happened, but I trusted. I trusted that God knows things that I do not know. His ways and thoughts are higher than mine:

"'For my thoughts are not your thoughts, neither are your ways My ways,'" declares the Lord. "'For as the heavens are higher than the earth, so are My ways higher than your ways, and my thoughts than your thoughts…'" — Isa. 55:8-9

"And we know that God causes all things to work together for good to those who love God, to those who are called according to His purpose." — Rom. 8:28

"He who dwells in the shelter of the Most High will abide in the shadow of the Almighty." — Ps. 91:1

I have hope. I have the hope of heaven. We all have the hope of heaven. All the secrets of the universe are found in Jesus Christ:

"…All the wealth comes from the full assurance of understanding, resulting in a true knowledge of God's mystery, that is Christ Himself, in whom are hidden all the treasures of wisdom and knowledge." — Col. 2:2-3

I want to share this with parents, grandparents, aunts, and uncles who have lost a child at any age, brothers and sisters who have lost a brother or sister, sons and daughters who have lost a parent or grandparent, husbands and wives who have lost their spouse, friends who have lost a friend, and anyone who has lost anyone. I lost my adult child. I remember him as a baby, a toddler, a child, an adolescent, a young adult, and a friend. I must use my son's name, Brian; but you could substitute the name of your loved one who you miss beyond words. If these letters in journal form can help you express your innermost feelings, bring them to the surface, and release them a little at a time, then that is my aim:

"Blessed be the God and Father of our Lord Jesus Christ, the Father of mercies and God of all comfort; who comforts us in all our affliction so that we may be able to comfort those who are in any affliction with the comfort with which we ourselves are comforted by God. For just as the sufferings of Christ are ours in abundance, so also our comfort is abundant through Christ." — 2 Cor. 1:3-5

I wrote the only words that could express my feelings to Brian. The words came out of my spirit and my relationship with God. As I reread my words, I noticed that so many of my ideas came from the Bible, although I may not have realized it at the time. I have found the verses in the Bible that pertain to those original thoughts and feelings. Since I did not write them at the time, I have included them at the end. I have also attached numbers of reference to the journal entries that correspond with the verses. I added many Bible verses that have been very comforting and helped me to think positively and receive His love and joy. May they uplift your soul and draw you closer to Him who will save you and will never leave you:

"My soul, wait in silence for God only, for my hope is from Him. He only is my rock and my salvation, my stronghold; I shall not be shaken." — Ps. 62:5-6

"…I am with you always, even to the end of the age." — Matt. 28:20

"And though you have not seen Him, you love Him, and though you do not see Him now, but believe in Him, you greatly rejoice with joy, inexpressible and full of glory, obtaining as the outcome of your faith the salvation of your souls." — 1 Pet. 1:8-9

When you see "fear Him," it does not mean to be afraid of Him; it means to have ultimate respect and reverence for Him.

Initially after Brian died, a friend of mine gave me the book, *Jesus Calling*. I thank God for the author, Sarah Young, whose inspired words reached my soul. God spoke to me and taught me His love through them.

Lord, I don't know how You love every single one of us so much. I only know that You do, and I am so thankful. I know that love cannot be measured, and that it can grow and stretch to infinity and still never break. I learned this because of each child and grandchild that was born. I know this because of my immeasurable love for them. You are love. God IS love. I am thankful.

"…For I will turn their mourning into joy, and will comfort them, and give them joy for their sorrow." — Jer. 31:13

"For I am convinced that neither death, nor life, nor angels, nor principalities, nor things present, nor things to come, nor powers, nor height, nor depth, nor any other created thing, shall be able to separate us from the love of God, which is in Christ Jesus our Lord." — Rom. 8:38-39

"God is love, and the one who abides in love, abides in God, and God abides in Him. We love, because He first loved us." — 1 John 4:16, 19

I believe that, as Brian is with God, and God is with me, then Brian is with me, too.

Christians have hope, the hope of heaven, faith in all knowledge in absolute Truth who is Jesus Christ. Heaven is the next place we go to live. Life on earth is temporal, but life in heaven is eternal:

"While we look not at the things which are seen, but at the things which are nor seen; for the things which are seen are temporal, but the things which are not seen are eternal." — 2 Cor. 4:18

Christians have hope, the hope of heaven

I hope that Jesus' love shines through the words He gives me. He is the light:

"In Him was life, and the life was the light of men. And the light shines in the darkness, and the darkness did not comprehend it. [He] was the true Light which, coming into the world, enlightens every man." — John 1:4, 9

"Our" Beach

MY SON, ETERNITY IS OURS.
MY BRIAN, YOU ARE SO CLOSE TO ME NOW.

November 16, 2013

I wrote the following words beginning around November 16, 2013, the day after you passed away to heaven: the worst, most painful day of my life.

Walks on the Beach with Brian

I am so proud of you. I wish you could be walking on the beach with me and we were inspiring each other like we always used to. You will inspire me forever, Brian, and everything I do, I'll do for you. Maybe I'll even do some of the things you wanted to do, but can't now, like run races and climb mountains (and ski down them as well). However, I definitely can't do FINANCE! I'll try to learn about stock options though.)

You would love the waves today. They are HUGE. You wanted to learn to surf with your big, new, red surfboard. Today would have been great. Remember when you jumped in the freezing cold waves right after Hurricane Sandy, in October, 2012? You were just a dot surrounded by water. What an adventurous spirit you have.

December 3, 2013

Can I ever feel joy again through this sorrow? Christmas joy through sorrow? I wish it is possible, but I don't see how, when I only feel like crying every second.

I'm going to run the Gloucester race for you. I'm going to get in shape and lose weight for you.

You'd enjoy Harper now. She's making such cute sounds. I always thought you'd be coming here to watch Gabby and Harper with me.

"Blessed are those that mourn, for they shall be comforted." — Matt. 5:4

But when? Maybe family and friends are comforting: they are for sure a form of comfort; their care has been amazing, but nothing and no one can bring you back to me. My limited mind thinks of the finality of it all and that it will take "forever" to see you again.

From what I can see, every day of the rest of my life is going to be torture, since I miss you every second of every day and I can't see you, hear you or touch you. You are front and center in my mind, though. I do know you are alive with the Lord. I pray every day for my mom and dad, Aunt Estelle, Grandma St. Cyr, Scott's mom, and Jesus to take good care of you.

I know God knows what it feels like to lose a son, and Mary does, too. Jesus, the only one to defeat death and the first to arise from it, however, rose in three days. I know we have the same promise of eternal life; but when a loved one dies, to us, it SEEMS like forever before we'll be able to see them again, even though it may not feel long to God. That's why it seems so final and devastating. God the Father only had to wait three days. We have to wait for the rest of our days on earth. It's more than I can bear right now.

I don't know why God has given us this burden to bear the rest of our lives. 32, 37, 42, 53

My darling, my sweetheart: I love you so much and miss you so much, from the deepest depths of my soul. I long to see you, eons more than anything I've ever wanted in my life, with my whole being. The wait seems longer than I can stand. I'd rather be cursed by a million plagues than to not have you here with me.

I only hope you know how much I love you and I hope you can feel it right now.

December 11, 2013

My dearest Brian,

I can't believe you're not here to talk with. Sometimes I wish I weren't alive, the pain of missing you is so severe. I wish I could see you in heaven; but I love your dad and sister and brothers, so I wouldn't leave them. I wouldn't want them to have to be doubly sad, either. They are all hurting deeply. I will have to wait to see you. 32

My face is always wet. I can't stop the tears. They are only the outward eruption of the deep soul-wrenching pain within me. Your laugh, your eyes, our talks, our fun, our socializing, the way you always help me, your funny ways of expressing affection, the pain of your dreams not being fulfilled, the broken heart of Stephen who wanted you in his daughters' lives, indescribable heartache, overwhelming sorrow giving way to mournful tears. I'm so proud of you, my Brian. I hope you know how much I love you. It's gushing out of me now: all these years happy to remain within me as a glowing face, a full heart, a lively step, and expressions of motherly affections.

There is no comfort for this mother. Every time I shed sorrowful tears from great gut passion pangs, my legs and arms get a rush of something that feels like I just had a shot of whisky, or, in my case, two sips of wine.

You just got your Master's Degree in Finance. You're the smartest guy around. You wanted a car and a house and a wife and kids, and to be an uncle. You adored Gabby and Harper. You still do. You can help them from where you are. You are much closer than we insecure earthlings think. Another realm; not so far away. All your dreams... makes me so extremely sad every time I think that you didn't even get a chance to do them... makes me the saddest of all... I am so sad and I feel the pain of Stephen right now.

Oh, please Brian: come back, please come back, please come back now.

Oh, my Brian, my baby, my Brian, my Brian, my Brian...infinity.

If my tears had the power to bring you back right now, you'd be standing before me... and I'd be happy again. Why the Lord wants us to have this pain, I don't know. I trust Him and love Him. Oh, Brian, are you with Him? Are you happy? Are you rejoicing? When we are all together in heaven, then I'll be rejoicing.

I'm looking for you, searching for you. Everywhere I go, show me you're here. I'll believe every sign you send. I need a hundred times more faith; no, a million times more...

GOD IS LOVE. Remember when we cried together? Yes, you do; remember when I said, "This is love. I can feel it;

God IS love." Brian, God gave us these special moments and many more this past year. It was a gift. He gave it to me because He knew what I didn't know: that it would be our last year together. We grew so close this year and did so many things together. I am so thankful for this. 97

I can't seem to get well. I have a sore throat and a cold and all this crying is taking its toll. It's aging me quickly, I'm afraid. I just don't see how I'll ever be happy again. If I get to 50% someday, that will probably be the best I can hope for. Right now, I can function on the outside when there are people around, but I'm so very sick on the inside. Some people may think it's over in a few days, weeks, or months. It's not. I guess it's better than the first few days, but in some ways, worse because it's getting deeper. I don't know.

Oh, my Brian, the perceptive one...

· ·

December 13, 2013

Oh, BRIAN,
Can you hear me?
Are you near me?

It is so hard walking around with a broken heart.

Twenty-nine months old or twenty-nine years old: doesn't matter, you'll always be my baby.

The thought of not seeing you the rest of my life just kills me. I have SICK HEART disease. Sometimes I think I'm getting better. Sometimes I think I'm getting worse.

....

December 14, 2013

My soul is tormented. Deep pangs of anguish arise from the depths of my soul longing to comfort you and be with you. I am in mourning. I am grief-stricken.

How happy they all must be in heaven to see you! How can they be so happy when they see how sad I am? Is it my choice to be this way? I don't think so. I have limited capabilities as a human.

Maybe our worlds are very close. Maybe when we sleep, we are half way between here and there. Maybe you woke up there instead of here, but maybe we're not far apart. Maybe you have alternate capabilities now than what I have.

You will meet the Father. Wow!

A mother's love to protect and care for her children is powerfully strong. I am beside myself that I couldn't protect you from this, or be with you to comfort you. This is absolutely what makes me the saddest. That, and you didn't get to live your dreams. These are my most grievous woes. I can't see you and talk with you. I can't hear your laugh that I love so much. We can't joke and play around. We can't share deep thoughts and cry together like we did.

I'm getting throat cramps. My throat is constantly sore. Every time I cry, my throat gets sore, and since I cry often every day, it's always sore. I'm all stuffed up and my eyes get puffy and wrinkly after I cry. I'm a mess. There's no perk in my step nor carefreeness in my voice or manner. I've a very sick heart. This burden is so heavy.

Maybe I will find peace someday. Even if I do, I will miss you incredibly, forever. You are part of me, my sweet son. I always called you "my sweet Brian." Your hair was so soft when you were a baby: I called you "Fluffy."

Oh, my baby, you were the best person anyone could be, and still are. I can't wait to see you. I miss you so much. When you're in heaven, do you miss people? Hmmm, I wonder if you miss me as much as I miss you.

The crux of the matter is that I see your clothes; but you're not in them, and it's killing me. I see your things; but you're not here, and it's killing me.

. . . .

January 4, 2014

It's the most lost and empty feeling to know I can never have you back, never see you again. Brian, it is

ABSOLUTELY THE WORST FEELING EVER, with no exaggeration.

It's why I need a hundred times more faith than I have. I have to believe that I will see you again. That life on earth is short, and we'll be rejoicing in heaven when we see each other again. God just wouldn't leave us all here to die. He wouldn't. He couldn't. He PROMISED. I need to look it up again. 45-48, 54, 91

Oh, my Brian. You're my sweetheart. I love you so much and miss you so much. It's indescribable. My treasure. God's greatest gift, a child—MY child—gone from me for the rest of my life: it's more than I can bear. Was this actually God's will? I need to understand more. 17

....
_____

January 7, 2014

All I can look at is your picture.
All I can touch is glass.
I can hear your laughter in my mind.
I can imagine myself touching your face. I see the details I know so well: your hair and eyelashes, your handsome eyes and eyebrows.
I can imagine putting my arms around you for a giant bear hug.

January 15, 2014

I have cared for you for 10,750 days, including 7 leap year days. A week of leap year days may not seem like much, but I included them because I'd give anything just to spend one more moment with you and that's 10,080 more minutes I'd be in heaven with you. I spent 250 days waiting for you to arrive. Then I cared for you for every moment of every day: through babyhood, toddler days, school days, summer days, graduations, our proudest moments, Holy Days, and ordinary days. I worried, laughed, cried, enjoyed the joyful times, and not many tough times. Now I cry through the "after you left us" days: every day, every moment, in my crushed heart; You've been gone from us 62 days today (my age), and I'll count each day on earth until I see you again...my sweet Brian.

Forever in our hearts, Brian, you are always with us. Running with us, skiing, golfing, playing, gaming, sporting, walking, climbing mountains, eating, horsing around, hanging out, and joking with us. ALWAYS WITH US. BEING WITH US. We miss you so much. You are part of each of us, the part that has been torn away; however, we cannot live without you. That is why you are close, so very close, to each of our hearts.

I miss our times driving home together, after watching Gabby and Harper, eating dinner out on the way home, and our talks. I miss the Watertown/ Somerville days. I miss you being home with us. I miss you.

I wanted to hug you and hold you when I found out you died. I had to wait a few days before I could. I was ready to burst. Utterly, these were the saddest days of my life. I wonder what happened to you on your way to heaven: what did you experience? At your wake, I was finally able to hold you the best I could. You are now held in a permanent hug for the rest of my life. You are so close to my heart. I am never without you, my beloved son, my buddy, my comrade, my inspiration.

You will never be just a memory. You are alive within each of us, living each day with us. You will be with us in everything we do. We are ALL together.

. . . .

January 22, 2014

This pain and grief will always be with me. It is a matter of learning to cope and coexist with the sorrow I carry within me.

Oh, my Brian, my baby, my buddy: I love you and miss you so much; infinitely more than words can express, from the bottom of my grievous heart. You are with me every day, every moment. My faith must be ultra-strong now. I BELIEVE I will hug you again someday and look into your handsome eyes. I remember your face ever so clearly. I see it every day. I listen to your laugh every day. I feel the pain of missing you and the joy of knowing you every day.

No more fun times with you on earth. This is what I miss the most: our fun times together. I'm looking forward to fun times in heaven: REJOICING to be in your presence again. Oh, how I wish you could answer me. 74

My stock options expired before I knew it. They were going to, of course, but I didn't know when. Only you knew so much about this; no one else does. I had to sell them. Now, I have some stock, but not options. I might educate myself, but I'll never have your knack or know-how. No one will. Maybe I'll make you proud of me. Neil gave me two thick mega books of yours to read on the subject. I'll update you—well, I guess you'll already know because you are with me always, like God. If He can listen and speak to me, you can too, right?

My BRIAN, always in my heart

BRIAN, ALWAYS IN OUR HEARTS

FOREVER WITH US

January 28, 2014

If I try to not think about you, I can function and be with people; but the minute I remember, everything comes back to me and the hurt is exactly the same. Without exaggerating, I can honestly say that being without you is torturous agony. It stings! I'd rather be stung by a thousand bees.

This is an irredeemable nightmare...but wait—my faith can set me free. Jesus Christ has promised us eternal life through Him, to those who believe. He is my Savior. He will carry my burden. In Him we live. I will see you again.

It's almost too hard to comprehend. It seems so unbearably long to this small mind of mine. It seems like I'll have to wait forever, but I BELIEVE that it won't actually be forever. 46-47, 51

> The words cannot be found to express my feelings. They do not exist. Maybe that is why my soul needs to meet another soul who feels the same way.

I just miss you so much and I long for you. You can see these words and read them, but you'll never know the gut-wrenching, nauseating feeling behind them unless I tell you, which I am, but the words cannot be found to express my feelings. They do not exist. Maybe that is why my soul needs to meet another soul who feels the same way. 69

February 12, 2014

Hi Brian, my Brian,

I think of you every day. In fact, I "wear" you. You and God. You clothe me. I'm wrapped up in you. The other day, I was thinking that I have more than enough sorrow to fill up wells and wells of tears yet to be shed. I can hear you say, "Don't be silly, Mom." That makes me laugh a little, but my dear, seriously, it's true.

The last week or so has been agony every day. It's because I was doing a lot of "Brian" stuff, like taking care of your clothes and writing thank you notes. Oh, my goodness, no one has any possible idea how difficult this is unless they go through it themselves. I'm never going to get over this. I'm never going to stop missing you.

Yesterday, during Gabby and Harper's nap time, I had to make calls to people to close some of your accounts, like Capitol One and Verizon. It was so sad... Huntington Theater, Red Cross, CVS. I hate turning off your phone. I always think of the last play we went to last summer; your gift to me for Mother's Day. It makes me smile a little to know that you were always trying to give me the best gift. You were always so thoughtful and you wanted to show me that you cared. Remember the fifty bucks you gave me in the card the year before? You knew that's what I wanted. You even said so. Every time I visit CVS, it reminds me of you.

I feel so bad about this: there were quite a few ladies who wanted to meet you on *Plenty of Fish*, even as recently as yesterday. Now, you'll never get the chance to meet them or get married or have children and a big house like you wanted. They were cute and seemed nice, too, some probably better matches than others. I told you that you have a lot to offer. You wrote on your profile that your work was your joy.

All your friends thought you were so funny. You were! Now, we imagine what you would say, and we can get a chuckle; but only you were the real thing, and what a wonderful sense of humor you HAVE. I guess your heavenly buddies are enjoying you now!

I hope you can see us and hear us and feel us. I just don't think memories were made to be forgotten and I don't think God would make them so special and then snatch them away. They are still with us always, even in heaven, I believe. 54

Oh, my baby boy. If any mother would think about how she nurtures her baby every moment of every day, then multiply it throughout childhood, even into college and getting on one's feet as a young adult—then no words can express the enormity of care that is put into that nurturing investment of love. It's too huge to be measured. Your worth is invaluable. Yes, God's most precious gift is a child. That is why it is the greatest loss. The depth of my feelings of loss for you is a fathomless chasm. It is impossible to measure: so is my love. It is INFINITE, like God. 17

I feel bad for all the people with broken hearts who sorely miss you: Dad, Christa, Stephen and Nicole, Neil, Grandpa, the family, all your close friends and work friends. Yes, you are a gift: we are so blessed to know you. You made the world wonderful for the people in your life.

I've got to get the girls now: they're crying, like me.

• •

February 13, 2014

Hi Brian,

I'm home now. I thought I closed your phone account, but you just got a text message from a girl writing, "hi there :)." Now, I see there are several more who want to meet you. This is so devastatingly sad to me that you can't respond, that you didn't get a chance to live and meet someone. It just makes me so sad for you and for them because they can't meet you. You would have been the best boyfriend, husband, and father in the world, and now you can't have that chance. It's wrenching my gut, my "well" where all my tears come from; that vast depth of emotion that thoughts like these pull up in buckets. I'm sobbing with feelings for your loss. I know you're in heaven now, and happy (I pray and hope); but still, I would have liked to see you happy here on earth first, too. Maybe it's just my limited mind wishing for these things for you, unable to comprehend the joy you must feel being with your Heavenly Father and Brother, but still, again, life on earth is precious, too, and God created it to be that way, right?

Oh, my dear love
Love you forever
Forever in my heart

There will be so much rejoicing in heaven when I see you again.

Oh, God, take good care of my baby 'til then.

. . . .

February 23, 2014

Hi Brian,

I am taking great pride in writing your full name each time on the front of these acknowledgement cards. That's at least one thing I can do. A beautiful name it is:

BRIAN KEITH ST. CYR. A wonderful name for a wonderful baby, boy, and man.

I often call out your name, or I speak it softly, or I cry for my baby: "my baby," always my baby. You probably don't want me calling you "baby," as you're a grown man. Please bear with me, though, and make an allowance for a mother's solemn perspective. Thanks.

I need to return to the cards. Some of them make me cry again. Your friends wrote so many honorable characteristics about you.

I love you with a deep, fathomless love. "I have loved you with an everlasting love," says the Lord in Jeremiah. 29

I want to read the Book of Job again. I'll let you know what it says.

By the way, I was talking with your friend, Jimmy, today via Facebook messaging. What a great friend he is; he thinks of you as his brother.

Living with sadness
What a broken heart I have

· ·

March 4, 2014

Sometimes, I am so sad, it makes me feel sick.

March 12, 2014

Four months have gone by. I may have climbed out of my well of tears, but I'm still sitting on the edge. I can fall in at any moment.

Perhaps I will see beyond the well to a blue and pink sky in the far distance: that is the hope I have from searching for it everywhere. I have just let friends comfort me. I'm on a different level now, closer to God than ever, from my need to know you're alright.

Oh, Brian, you are so very close to my heart; nothing can separate us. I can't wait to see you, but I have to. I don't understand, but I trust. I told you that you were very special, remember? (You said "thank you.") God wants you with Him now. I guess you're even closer to Him there in heaven than here. 13, 70

Neil appears to be alright, but I believe that's only because he hasn't gone deep enough into his soul to feel the pain. For me, that's where I started. I can understand why a 23-year-old would have a difficult time doing this; however, whatever he is doing seems to be working for him. In some ways, a mother understands her child better than anyone, even as he grows older into adulthood—but no one can know another's heart completely, except God. God and the human heart: closer than anyone, more intimate than marriage. Dad and I are closer than ever, too.

Each of us understands the pain the other feels. YOU, our creation in union with God, were *nurtured for a lifetime... cared for... trained... guided... loved... laughed with... cried with... treasured...* Our part is over; I wish it wasn't that way, but it's God's way, not mine. God's creation in union with us. I guess you always belonged to God; but you belong to us, too. God knows it will always be that way. He wouldn't just take you from us. It's up to us to try and understand. God, our loving God, created you for us and for Himself. If nothing can separate us from the love of God, then nothing can separate us from you, either. I believe that. That means that our trust and faith will get us through until we can see you again.

> If nothing can separate us from the love of God, then nothing can separate us from you, either.

The spiritual world is even better than this one, so I've heard. It must be immensely so; I imagine that earthly love is MAGNIFIED—not a hundred, a thousand, or a million times, but an infinite number of times, and each number multiplied infinitely beyond that. That's a lot of love. I feel that in my heart for you. I hope my other children realize that I love them that much, too. I can't believe how stretchable love is, but I learned that each time one of you was born. 71

LOVE WAS BORN.
Jesus IS Love.
God IS Love.

A different level: I now know that earth is a place where we spend a short period of time. God shows many glimpses of heaven to all of us every day. (Oh, I feel so sorry for those that can't see it, hear it, or feel it.) Earth itself is a wonder to treasure; but most of all, each person shows us glimpses of God, who lives within each heart. Eternity: that is the place to be. Forever. And ever. Rejoicing forever. In the vastness of His shining Love.

On earth, we are like seeds being planted in the soil, breaking open, rooting and growing up toward the "Son." When we burst forth, we become the true selves we were meant to be; that is our birth, our death, our freedom into the wide-open grandeur of our new realm: heaven, in all its glory! 57, 78 paragraph 2; (verse 36)

> Eternity: that is the place to be. Forever. And ever. Rejoicing forever. In the vastness of His shining Love.

March 14, 2014

Today is Dad's birthday. I guess you already know that. Missing you is agony. Please send me a hug from heaven.

April 30, 2014

Hi, my Brian,

I cry for you every day. Whenever I think of you ALIVE, it's like you ARE ... and then... I realize you're not... and that tears me up inside. I still just cannot believe that you're not here...

I just can't believe it...

I just can't believe it...

I am doing better on the outside: I am coping and enjoying family and friends, but your absence is always with me; your loss is present all the time. I'm always in pain on the inside, but you are not to know this, I guess. I was on the beach the other day and (in case you didn't hear me) I begged God to tell you I love you and miss you from the depths of my being. He gave me a rock in the shape of a heart IMMEDIATELY after, so I cried because I knew He would tell you! I love you so much. Some people say that there is no connection between the loved ones who have gone to heaven, and the souls still here on earth, but does anyone really know? So, I guess I can believe what I want, and I like to believe you are near, so I do. If, after more Biblical research about heaven, I discover new information, then I'll adjust my thinking accordingly and I'll let you know!

I JUST CAN'T DESCRIBE how much I miss you, though! It's so immensely, deeply, and infinitely permeating the essence of my spiritual being. We are one. Our family together: we are one.

MY GREATEST TREASURE IS LOST.

I just want to be reunited with you! To have us all together again!

Remember Neil's graduation dinner at that restaurant? I said, "I love it when we are all together," because it is such a blessing to me and always made me feel so proud and full of pure joy. It will never be the same again... you will always be missing.

But we, all of us, must always keep in mind that you are strongly present with us... you will never be without us; you are within us.

You will always be with us… talking, joking, laughing, making fun of me and my "mothering mistakes," which were VERY FEW, by the way! I miss playing, eating, loving, living!! What an awesome, UNITED family we were...ARE!

I'm going to read and learn more about heaven. I read *To Heaven and Back*, by Mary Neal. There's a movie out called *Heaven Is for Real*; I must see it.

God is always my strength, my peace, my comfort. The meaning of life is much GRANDER than most earthlings think. 23

My wound, my sorrow, will never be a scar. It will always be open and bleeding, a perpetual wound; but it's not on the skin, it's in the heart: my living, sad, crying heart. The sorrow lives next to the joy, both within the same heart. 30

....

May 2, 2014

<u>This Heart Fell in Love</u> (The eyes of my mind and heart see each event.)

These eyes saw you for the first time
These hands held your tiny head
These ears heard your cries
These arms held you close
This heart fell in love

These eyes looked into yours
This heart filled with joy

These eyes watched you grow
These hands held you up
These ears heard you play
These arms hugged your wounds
This heart filled with love

These eyes read your homework, watched you block, ride
your bike, run uphill, win the race
This heart cheered you on
This heart filled with joy

These eyes watched you graduate
These ears heard your name
These arms embraced you
This heart burst with pride and joy

This heart remembers our walks, the beach, the hikes,
    our talks, our holidays, the plays
    the waves, the snow, the slopes.

These hands cupped your face,
    touched your soft hair, eyebrows, and eyelashes for
    the last time

This heart burst and broke

This mind sees your face, your smile,
Hears your voice, your laugh
Hugs you
Every day.
This heart fell in love
This heart fills with joy and sorrow

This heart is filled with riches and treasures, of love
and memories

Just for you:

This heart remembers the Gnomes and Sebastian, Montessori, McDonald's, and Shaw's.
It remembers Disney, Cheverus, Blue Man Group, Boston times, The Statue of Liberty,
Federal Jacks, golf, Tin-Tin, a sunburn, *Settlers of Catan*…

Our last phone conversation: twenty-six minutes, which was the very last…

• •
___

May 10, 2014

I can feel it physically. It goes from an empty, hole-crushing feeling in my chest to my brain, which then stings in my head, comes out my eyes in tears, then permeates throughout my limbs, weakening them. This is the expression of sorrow.

It takes my breath away, fills my head with congestion, makes my shoulders heave… and then the sorrow returns to the heart and it begins all over again. My face is wet. This is how sorrow feels.

• •
___

May 28, 2014

My baby,
If love can transcend realms, you can feel mine now. Close, close to my heart are you and will always be.

Mothers' Day was hard. You gave me a gift. It is a B-shaped heart necklace with "mom" engraved on it. It is precious to me as it represents our love. It is close to my heart when I wear it. I love you.

We went on a retreat to Delaware with Billy Perkins (the priest who baptized you on the banks of the Hudson River) and Varghese and Rani. We stayed at "Jesus House."

Billy spoke of life, death, and resurrection: the cycle of life and our "spiritual DNA." We were with our closest friends and there was intimate sharing and comfort. It was a precious gift from God.

Right now, we are visiting Christa in California. You are always with us.

....

June 9, 2014

Your Birthday.

The depth of my soul is an ocean.
Sitting above it, I feel no pain.

July 10, 2014

How can I go on each day? Coping is the bandage covering this perpetually bleeding spiritual heart. I am a soul living here on earth.

There are many paths that lead to the middle of my heart where you live, with God. I walk on some of them each day and I find you. They are very short paths, just a couple of steps, really. A path can be a song, a word, your hat, a memory, one of your sibling's laughs, a gift you gave me, or talking about you and remembering things you said, and so many more reminders. I found your ski jacket with the lift ticket still attached; the last day you ever went skiing. I buried my head in your coat and cried.

My truly significant hope is seeing you in eternity. 5, 32

August 16, 2014

I'm living on the surface of my heart.

My heart is an ocean. I cope by living on the surface of it, like being on a sailboat. Everywhere I go, you hold me up. You are with God. You are together. To reach you, I only touch the surface of the water. My fingers dip below the surface, attached to my hand above; or, my hand submerges, attached to my arm. Sometimes, I am completely submerged, thoroughly wet with tears for love of missing you. Oh, my soul. Nothing can separate us from our love, the bonded love of God. We are part of each other. Our love is eternally entwined. 71

> My truly significant hope is seeing you in eternity.

I am only human, grieving the way a human does. Part of me is missing—not really, but it feels that way. We all feel that part of our family is missing. It's you: you are the missing part. Your friends miss you, too. You are part of them, too. They cared about you, Brian. I wish you had another chance to live. I know you live now in a more glorious way. I trust that our Heavenly Father knows what's best for you, even if I don't understand. We will all be together again; but for now, it seems like it will take so long. You are always with us.

I'm at the beach now. The thought of missing you cuts to my core again. You are with me every day, every moment.

....

September 24, 2014

It's been ten months since you went to live in the next place; our forever home.

I lost my baby, my handsome boy, and the pain is so great. I still cry every day for you. If God keeps our tears in a bottle, He would need a canyon for mine. So very many things remind me of you: your hat, your shoes, gifts you gave me, pictures, memories, walks on the beach, Thanksgiving joy around the table, football, (your favorite, and those games with dad and your brothers), Christmas laughter, and a thousand other thoughts. You are constantly with me in my heart, and I can't wait until we are all together again. 11

I posted a picture on Facebook of *the last time we were all together at the same time*. It was the day after Billy and Sue's wedding, August 25, 2013, in Stowe, Vermont. We were all having brunch together. This makes me the saddest of all. I know you're with us and we'll be together again, but it's so hard not having you here physically.

> Thank goodness God saves me every day with His love, peace, joy and comfort. All I want is to be close to Him, so I spend time alone with Him each day.

Thank goodness God saves me every day with His love, peace, joy and comfort. All I want is to be close to Him, so I spend time alone with Him each day. It's the only thing getting me by, along with the comfort of friends He sends my way. I feel sorrow for my other children and husband who are also suffering, along with your friends. I hope we all become closer to God. 23

October 5, 2014

The pain isn't any less now. I've just learned to surf on the surface of my ocean heart.

__The first year has gone by.__

My Brian Star

January 13, 2015

My heart has written so much more that I have not put into words here.

If my heart is an ocean, my life is like walking on water.

My greatest HOPE is HEAVEN: I'm reading many books to help grow my faith.

I want to get a tiny desk for my bedroom to write to you and God.

God, you're calling me to more than I am.

I must start...

Brian Always With Me
BAWM
BAWU

Flowing river underground
Always full of pain
Except when you don't go there.

My life is like living on a glacier, with so many cracks and crevices to fall into my soul.

....

February 23, 2015

Be the presence in my emptiness.
Maybe spirits grow in their humanness.

March 5, 2015

Today is bleak and dreary, but the SON will come.

March 6, 2015

What is in my heart
    comes out my eyes
        and hurts my throat.

March 10, 2015

I'm sad all over on the inside.

I'm walking on glaciers with fissures, leading to the center of my soul. There are many crevices to my heart.

May 5, 2015

My heart is like the earth: I have a river of sorrow running through the middle that leads to the deepest sorrows I have ever felt, in the depths of the ocean of my soul. The rest of my heart has ridges, crags, mountains, valleys, trees, grass, and paths. The most important presence in my heart is the SON shining through all of it.

....

May 6, 2015

My heart box has a cover.
Inside there is a river of sorrow running through the middle.
Outside there is laughter.
Inside there is joy on the banks of the river where my loved ones make memories with me.
Outside there is friendly chatter. These are good times with friends and family.
Inside there is joy and peace surrounding my river, a strong comfort through faith and trust.

....

June 9, 2015 (your birthday)

There's a river of love flowing through me, water of sorrow.

The banks are green; but, lest they become saturated and my whole heart turns into one big river, the river must be contained, so that happiness can dwell on the grass.

The river must stay in the middle of my heart, where it first broke in half.

· ·

September 14, 2015

Greatest treasure
Beyond measure
My heart hurts into my throat.

I'm holding hands with my son's heart, walking along the beach.

· ·

September 22, 2015

I just cover up the pain by doing things; but really, it's like there's a dagger stuck in my heart. My God is giving me peace and joy, however. I saved your pillow case in my box. My faith and KNOWING that I'll see you again keeps me living in the Hope of Heaven. The presence of His light shining on me and warming my life is what keeps me alive. 3, 6, 60, 66

December 4, 2015

Sad, but lovely.
Sad, but peaceful.
Sad, but joyful.

The second year has gone by.

January 13, 2016

I will never be finished crying my tears for you.

I hold your heart in my hand; I hold your heart in my heart.

God is closer to me than the air I breathe. He is with you also, at the same time. That means we are together. 7, 65

The day I see you again, joy will be overflowing my heart like I have never known. 72, 74

March 24, 2016

The Lord is always beside me. I walk and walk and I look up and see that His light is still with me. I turn around and walk the other way and His light is still beside me.

Brian,

There's a hole in our lives. There's a big hole in each of our lives. There's a huge hole in our family. There's an empty hole in my heart. It's being filled with Jesus' love.

Sometimes, the treasure you take away from the beach is in your heart.

> God is closer to me than the air I breathe. He is with you also, at the same time. That means we are together.

September 27, 2016

I had this thoughtful revelation as I walked the beach yesterday morning: if God provides such lovely shell homes to creatures such as the clams of the sea, then we can be certain that He will give us homes in heaven, as He loves us much more than crabs and scallops. He has made each of us an individual whom He loves dearly. He wouldn't just leave us, our souls, to die.

***The third year has gone by.**ic*

His Glory, Unedited

February 24, 2017

Brian,

Every time I tell you that I miss you so much, it is only one drop in the ocean of how much I really miss you.

God,

If you breathed life into us when we were born, then that life does not go away because it is life itself, which is You, God. Our bodies of flesh and blood, although a miracle, die—but our spirits are always living. You are the God of life and light. Death and darkness cannot put out the light. 44, 50, 96

March 2, 2017

Perhaps our spirits are who we are as people and our souls are who we are with God.

I'm going to plant seeds to symbolize how God has planted us on earth. As seeds burst forth into full bloom, so too will we when we are born into heaven.

Life is a cycle. Everything that seems dead, comes alive again. 57, 78

. . . .

March 28, 2017

When I look up at all the gray clouds, I see the "Son."

First the clouds, then the joy.

First Lent, then Easter.

> Life is a cycle. Everything that seems dead, comes alive again.

Our hope is in the joy behind the clouds: the "Son."

We should give the hope that is in You, as well as receive it.

. . . .

September 28, 2017

I fell in to my ocean of sadness beneath the glacier. I slipped through the crevice of your love where love has no bottom or sides.

I can't "move on" with my life, but I can _move with you_ always in my heart.

November 7, 2017

Brian,

Since you died, I've been living somewhere between heaven and earth.

My perspective is from a viewpoint higher than the surface of the earth, like being on a high mountaintop, your favorite place.

I love you.

December 23, 2017

I have never been so joyful
in my life.
I have never been so sorrowful
in my life.

Together, they live beside each other in my heart:
joy, because I am closer to God than ever before;
sorrow, because I have been separated from my beloved son, Brian.

HUGS FROM HEAVEN

The hope of heaven keeps me alive. God, Your love for me overwhelms me, beyond my understanding, but I am so very thankful. 46, 66, 90, 92

I can see everyone in a new light: Your light, shining on them. I am so thankful. I see the goodness and the preciousness of each person, each Your creation, and the beauty and miracles all around.

"We live by faith, not by sight." — 2 Cor. 5:7

> The hope of heaven keeps me alive. God, Your love for me overwhelms me, beyond my understanding, but I am so very thankful.

"Miracles are not always visible to the naked eye, but those who live by faith can see them clearly. Living by faith, rather than sight, enables you to see My Glory." — Sarah Young, from entry December 21, "Jesus Calling"

The fourth year has gone by.

....

January 29, 2018

I have learned to live…
I am living on the surface of my ocean heart.

There is a river of sadness flowing through the crack where my heart broke. On the banks are trees of life and joy.

June 25, 2018

My dear Brian,

Whenever I think of you alive, it makes me hurt more, knowing you're not alive, but dead…
But then…
I turn and see *HOPE,* where you <u>are</u> alive.
You are always, always with us.

A couple of weeks ago, I worked in your room: hanging pictures, going through your books, yearbooks, trophies, baseball cards, etc. All this was difficult and, since your birthday was approaching, it got tough at times… Remembering all the good times made me happy; but then realizing the truth, made me sad. I couldn't stay in your room for more than an hour or two at a time.

I came across all of your diplomas and degrees. Your last greatest achievement on earth, was earning your Master's degree in finance, your mind's love, at Boston College. I am so glad we went to that all-day, double graduation ceremony and celebrated later by going out to dinner. The point is that it represents all that we worked for, your entire life: all the education, preparing for the world, all the nurturing, love and care, that we were beyond blessed to be able to do for you and with you. This degree represents all that. Thoughts of this touched my heart beyond measure. I took the degree (that you earned just a few months ago) to be professionally framed. It is now hanging on your wall, a meaningful symbol of your cherished life.

....

August 19, 2018

Everything is inspiration if you have eyes to see and ears to hear.

"Be still and <u>know</u> that I am God." – Psalm 46:10

Sorrow shows you joy.

Sometimes, it seems like the joy isn't as deep as the sorrow. Maybe we are meant to be joyful and not sorrowful.

....

September 7, 2018

I grieve with hope. 92

The fifth year has gone by.

February 15, 2019

Standing in the Son.
Moving in the Son.
Living in the Son.
Walking in the Son.

A broken heart is a more clearly cut heart.
A broken heart is cut deep.

. . . .

April 18, 2019

Trust and obey, and
you'll be okay!
Sorrow and joy are both from love.

. . . .

June 6, 2019

You and I, together with God, take many long walks along the beach in early morning. You are with me, so you know.

Here's what happened on May 30, and this is what I wrote:

Dear Brian,
I was walking along the beach. I was thinking of you and how your birthday is getting closer. It made me so sad. I took two steps and looked down. I saw a heart–shaped

piece of sea glass. I knew immediately it was from you. You said, "Mom, I'm right here with you." Then I looked down and saw a cradle-shaped heart. You'll always be my baby.

Heart tears today, my beloved.

The sixth year has gone by.

February 10, 2020

The other day (last week) while I was on the beach:

"Are you walking with me, Brian?" I look down and there's a big heart. Thank you.
Yes, I think: *I know we can't touch hands, but <u>we can touch our spirits</u>*. A little farther down the beach, a smaller heart tells me, "I'm still with you."

March 20, 2020

When I go in your room, you're there. I remember everything about you, and all the memories, and, my dear God, I love you.

All of us are missing something in our lives: you. An empty space, a large hole. Yet, you are always with us. On a different, spiritual plane, you are here.

Our faith binds us.
Our hope saves us.
Our love keeps us through eternity.

April 23, 2020

Living on the surface of my ocean heart, at any given moment, while thinking of you, my spirit plummets into the depths of the sea, as if teleported there.

. . . .

April 24, 2020

Sometimes, instead of plummeting deep into my soul, my soul erupts, bursting forth to consciousness like an underground geyser.

Either way, it's all my soul, my spirit loving you and missing you.

. . . .

May 25, 2020

Doing little things I enjoy keeps me from hurting too much, but you are <u>always</u> missing from us.

. . . .

June 9, 2020

Dear Brian,
Today is your birthday. We are so sad you are missing from us. It's been six and a half years you've been gone

HUGS FROM HEAVEN

from us. We know where you are, but we're just not sure where it is. The hope of heaven gives us strength. Our belief gets us through each day. 12, 90, 91, 92

We honored you today. Dad and I went to church: mass at St. Joe's. It was weird because of the pandemic. We had to wear masks, be escorted in, sit far from anyone else, etc.

Later, Neil joined us for breakfast at home. You'd like the bacon and eggs. Is there food in heaven? We then went for a hike at Edward Smith trail, mostly in Kennebunkport, off Guinea Road. I never even knew it was there. We were there about an hour and a half. Dad had to get back to work. Of course, you were walking with us. Later that evening, Dad and I looked through some pictures of you in photo albums in your room. I'm so sad thinking about how distraught it makes me, made me; but so happy to have had you, known you, know you, loved you, love you. The memories are treasures. The loss of future ones, is sad. We'll be together again in heaven, someday. 55, 58

All my love,
Mom

. . . .

October 28, 2020

The hurting sorrow is so very deep; deeper than the bottom of the ocean in the deepest part.

The seventh year has gone by.

March 16, 2021

Brian,

I can't see you.
I can't hear you.
I can't touch you,
But I can
Feel you
In my heart
Every day.

. . . .

November 14, 2021

Dear Brian,

I bought a beautiful orchid for the sanctuary at church today. It was in remembrance of you. Your name with our dedication to you was in the bulletin:

> "The altar flowers are given in loving memory of Brian St. Cyr, with love from Mom, Dad, Christa, Stephen and Nicole, and Neil."

You are always with us: in our thoughts and hearts.

The eighth year has gone by.

March 26, 2022

There is a violet by your grave. I noticed it there last fall. Every other flower had disappeared, but here was this tiny purple flower standing bravely in the grass. It was still there when the snow came. Now the winter has come and gone. I looked at the ground today, and the little violet is STILL THERE!

I am perplexed. I am in awe. This is the sweetest of miracles, one that could go by unnoticed, but I see it. What does this mean?!

Later, I learned that a violet represents FAITH. Its petals are heart shaped: it means LOVE, too.

Brian, you are here! I will see you again! FAITH brings the HOPE of heaven. You are LIVING!

"Faith is the assurance of things hoped for and the conviction of things unseen." — Heb. 11:1

Brian, I believe this is your special sign to me, allowed by God. Thank you!

July 13, 2022

Brian,

This is what I said to you as I stopped by your grave today: "Do you know how much I love you? Can you hear my words? Can you hear my heart?"

When I see you again, I'll be a better dancer than I've ever been!

My heart will swing through the trees over my joy of seeing you! 74

The ninth year has gone by.

August 2023

November 14, 2013 – November 14, 2023:

It has been ten years since a policeman knocked on our front door at 3:00 a.m. to inform us that "Keith has passed away."

I rocked myself back and forth on my bed, crazed, hoping against hope that it was a mistake. That they have the wrong person. Our son's name is Brian, although Keith is his middle name. This was, absolutely, the most rude awakening anyone could encounter. It was beyond rude. It made rude seem kind. It was an attack. I rocked myself back and forth, sobbing, and verbalizing something like prayers…I don't even remember…but for three hours, until early morning, when Dad and I drove to the beach two miles away. We walked on and on, out of our minds. A passersby could not know the pain we carried with us in those moments. We plodded on to the very edge of the end of the beach, then back to the other end. The world we had known no longer existed.

Time, for the next three years, became a non-reality.

He was our son!

Our hearts were torn in half, crushed.

The most devastating tragedy had occurred in our lives. His roommate had the police notify us. (Brian had fallen asleep. He didn't wake up here. He woke up in heaven. He met the Lord that night.)

··

November 2023

I can't read a single page of this without diving into the deep…

The tenth year has gone by.

HOPE

Ten years sounds like a long time, but it isn't. Time doesn't even exist when you've lost your loved one. God, however, does exist, and He is not held by time. Time does not exist for Him either. He is the Alpha and the Omega, the beginning and the end, and everything in between.

"…I am the Alpha and the Omega, the beginning and the end. I will give to the one who thirsts from the spring of the water of life without cost." — Rev. 21:6

> Time doesn't even exist when you've lost your loved one. God, however, does exist, and He is not held by time.

I have chosen some comforting and uplifting verses that I have personally found to be true. They will help you to see God's love for you, even when you are suffering. I have written them in the order in which they appear in the Bible. I have also attached the verse numbers to my original thoughts in the letters I wrote to Brian. The verses are from the *New American Standard Bible*, unless otherwise noted.

Then, I divided them into themes to help you quickly find solace and strength when you need it. The Bible is living because God speaks to you through it. Listening to and communing with God makes all the

> The Bible is living because God speaks to you through it. Listening to and communing with God makes all the difference in our lives.

difference in our lives. (Some verses have themes that may overlap.)

1   Deuteronomy 33:27
    "The eternal God is a dwelling place,
    And underneath are the everlasting arms..."

2   2 Samuel 22:29
    "For Thou art my lamp, O God;
    And the Lord illumines my darkness"

3   Nehemiah 8:10
    "...Do not be grieved, for the joy of the Lord is your strength."

4   Psalm 23:4
    "Even though I walk through the valley of the shadow of death, I fear no evil; for Thou art with me..."

5   Psalm 27:14
    Wait for the Lord;
    Be strong and let your heart take courage;
    Yes, wait for the Lord.

6   Psalm 31:14-15, 24
    "But as for me, I trust in Thee, O Lord,
    I say, "Thou art my God."
    My times are in Thy hand...
    Be strong, and let your heart take courage,
    All you who hope in the Lord."

7   Psalm 34:18
    "The Lord is near to the brokenhearted, and saves those who are crushed in spirit."

8   Psalm 42:5
    "Why are you in despair, O my soul?
    And why have you become disturbed within me?
    Hope in God, for I shall again praise Him for the help of His presence."

9   Psalm 46:1
    "God is our refuge and strength, a very present help in trouble."

10 Psalm 46:10
    "Cease striving [Be still–King James Version] and know that I am God."

11 Psalm 56:8
    "Thou hast taken account of my wanderings; put my tears in Thy bottle…"

12 Psalm 62:5-6
    "My soul, wait in silence for God only,
    For my hope is from Him.
    He only is my rock and my salvation,
    My stronghold; I shall not be shaken."

13 Psalm 62:8
    "Trust in Him at all times, O people;
    Pour out your heart before Him; God is a refuge for us."

14 Psalm 73:23-24
   "Nevertheless I am continually with Thee;
   Thou hast taken hold of my right hand.
   With Thy counsel Thou wilt guide me,
   And afterward receive me to glory."

15 Psalm 73:26
   "My flesh and my heart may fail,
   But God is the strength of my heart and my portion forever."

16 Psalm 91:1
   "He who dwells in the shelter of the Most High
   Will abide in the shadow of the Almighty."

17 Psalm 127:3
   "Behold, children are a gift of the Lord;
   The fruit of the womb is a reward."

18 Psalm 145:18-19
   "The Lord is near to all who call upon Him,
   To all who call upon Him in truth.
   He will fulfill the desire of those who fear Him in truth…"

19 Proverbs 3:5-6
   "Trust in the Lord with all your heart,
   And do not lean on your own understanding.
   In all your ways acknowledge Him,
   And He will make your paths straight."

20 Proverbs 3:21-22
"Keep sound wisdom and discretion, so they will be life to your soul…"

21 Proverbs 4:18
"But the path of the righteous is like the light of dawn, That shines brighter and brighter until the full day."

22 Proverbs 4:23
"Watch over your heart with all diligence, For from it flow the springs of life."

23 Isaiah 12:2
"Behold, the Lord is my salvation, I will trust and not be afraid; For the Lord God is my strength and my song, And He has become my salvation."

24 Isaiah 25:8
"He will swallow up death for all time, And the Lord God will wipe tears away from all faces…"

25 Isaiah 30:15
"For thus the Lord God, the Holy one of Israel, has said, 'In repentance and rest you shall be saved, In quietness and trust is your strength.'"

26 Isaiah 40:31
"Yet those who wait for the Lord will gain new strength; They will mount up with wings like eagles,

They will run and not get tired,
They will walk and not become weary."

27 Isaiah 44:6
"I am the first and I am the last,
And there is no God besides Me."

28 Isaiah 49:15-16
"Can a woman forget her nursing child, and have no compassion on the son of her womb?
Even these may forget, but I will not forget you.
Behold, I have inscribed you on the palms of My hands…"

29 Jeremiah 31:3
"I have loved you with an everlasting love;
Therefore I have drawn you with lovingkindness."

30 Jeremiah 31:13
"For I will turn their mourning into joy,
And will comfort them, and give them joy for their sorrow."

31 Jeremiah 31:17
"'And there is hope for your future', declares the Lord."

32 Lamentations 3:21-26
"Therefore I have hope. The Lord's loving-kindnesses indeed never cease,
For His compassions never fail.
They are new every morning;

Great is Thy faithfulness.
'The Lord is my portion', says my soul,
'Therefore I have hope in Him.'
The Lord is good to those who wait for Him, to the person who seeks Him."

33 Habakkuk 3:19
"The Lord God is my strength,
And He has made my feet like hinds' feet,
And makes me walk on my high places."

34 Zephaniah 3:17
"The Lord your God is in your midst, a victorious warrior.
He will exult over you with joy,
He will renew you in His love,
He will rejoice over you with shouts of joy."

35 Matthew 5:4
"Blessed are those who mourn, for they shall be comforted."

36 Matthew 11:28-30
"Come to Me all who are weary and heavy-laden, and I will give you rest.

Take My yoke upon you and learn from Me, for I am gentle and humble in heart; and you shall find rest for your souls, for My yoke is easy and My load is light."

37 Matthew 28:6-9
"'He is not here, for He has risen, just as He said. Come, see the place where He was lying. And go quickly and tell His disciples that He has risen from the dead; and behold, He is going before you into Galilee, there you will see Him; behold, I have told you.'
And they departed quickly from the tomb with fear and great joy and ran to report it to His disciples.
And behold, Jesus met them and greeted them. And they came up and took hold of His feet and worshiped Him."

38 Matthew 28:20
"...I am with you always, even to the end of the age."

39 Mark 16:6
"And He said to them, 'Do not be amazed; you are looking for Jesus, the Nazarene, who has been crucified. He has risen; He is not here; here is the place where they laid Him.'"

40 Luke 1:78-79
"The Sunrise from on high shall visit us, to shine upon those who sit in darkness and the shadow of death, to guide our feet into the way of peace."

41 Luke 23: 42-43
(One criminal on the cross said,) "'Jesus, remember me when you come into your kingdom!'" And He

said to him, 'Truly I say to you, today you shall be with Me in Paradise.'"

42 Luke 24 :6-8
"'He is not here, but He has risen. Remember how He spoke to you while He was still in Galilee, saying that the Son of Man must be delivered into the hands of sinful men, and be crucified, and the third day rise again.' And they remembered His words."

43 Luke 24: 12
But Peter arose and ran to the tomb; stooping and looking in, he saw the linen wrappings only; and he went away to his home, marveling at that which had happened.

44 John 1: 4, 9
"In Him was life, and the life was the light of men. And the light shines in the darkness, and the darkness did not comprehend it.
[He] was the true light which, coming into the world, enlightens every man."

45 John 1: 12-13
"But as many as received Him, to them He gave the right to become children of God, even to those who believe in His name, who were born not of blood, nor of the will of the flesh, nor the will of man, but of God."

46 John 3:16
"For God so loved the world, that He gave His only begotten Son, that whoever believes in Him should not perish, but have eternal life."

47 John 6:47
"Truly, truly I say to you, he who believes has eternal life."

48 John 6:51
"I am the living bread that came down out of heaven; if anyone eats of this bread, he shall live forever; and the bread also which I shall give for the life of the world is my flesh."

49 John 6:54-56
"He who eats my flesh and drinks My blood has eternal life, and I will raise him up on the last day… He abides in Me, and I in Him."

50 John 8:12
"Jesus spoke to them, saying, 'I am the light of the world; he who follows Me shall not walk in the darkness, but shall have the light of life.'"

51 John 8:31-32
"If you abide in My word, then you are truly disciples of Mine; and you shall know the truth, and the truth shall make you free."

52 John 10:14-15
"I am the good shepherd; and I know My own, and My own know Me, even as the Father knows Me and I know the Father; and I lay down My life for the sheep."

53 John 10:17-18
"For this reason the Father loves Me, because I lay down My life, that I may take it again. No one has taken it away from Me, but I lay it down on My own initiative. I have authority to lay it down, and I have authority to take it up again. This commandment I received from My Father."

54 John 10:27-30
"My sheep hear My voice, and I know them, and they follow Me; and I give eternal life to them, and they

shall never perish; and no one shall snatch them out of My hand.

My Father, who has given them to Me, is greater than all; and no one is able to snatch them out of the Father's hand. I and the Father are one."

55 John 11:25-26

"Jesus said to her (Martha), 'I am the resurrection and the life; he who believes in Me shall live even if He dies, and everyone who lives and believes in Me shall never die.'"

56 John 11:33, 35-36, 38, 40-44

"When Jesus therefore saw her weeping (Mary, over her brother, Lazarus, who had died), and the Jews who came with her, also weeping, He was deeply moved in spirit and was troubled. Jesus wept. And so the Jews were saying, 'Behold how much He loved Him!' Jesus therefore being deeply moved within, came to the tomb.

Jesus said to her, 'Did I not say to you, if you believe, you will see the glory of God?' ...

'Father, I thank Thee that Thou heardest Me. And I knew that Thou hearest Me always; but because of the people standing around I said it, that they may believe that Thou didst send Me.'

He cried out with a loud voice, 'Lazarus, come forth.' He who had died came forth, bound hand and foot... Jesus said to them, 'Unbind him and let him go.'"

57 John 12:24

"Truly, truly, I say to you, unless a grain of wheat falls into the earth and dies, it remains by itself alone; but if it dies, it bears much fruit."

58 John 14:1-3

"Let not your heart be troubled; believe in God, believe also in Me.

In My Father's house are many dwelling places (mansions – KJV); if it were not so, I would have told you; for I go to prepare a place for you.

And if I go and prepare a place for you, I will come again, and receive you to Myself, that where I am, there you may be also."

59 John 14:6

"I am the way, and the truth, and the life; no one comes to the Father, but through Me."

60 John 16:22

"Therefore you too now have sorrow; but I will see you again, and your heart will rejoice, and no one takes your joy away from you."

61 John 16:33

"These things I have spoken to you, that in Me you may have peace. In the world you have tribulation, but take courage; I have overcome the world."

62 John 17:3
"And this is eternal life, that they may know Thee, the only true God, and Jesus Christ whom Thou hast sent."

63 John 20:30-31
"Many other signs therefore Jesus also performed in the presence of the disciples, which are not written in this book; but these have been written that you may believe that Jesus is the Christ, the Son of God; and that believing you may have life in His name."

64 John 21:13-14
"Jesus came and took the bread, and gave them, and the fish likewise.

This is now the third time that Jesus was manifested to the disciples, after He was raised from the dead."

65 Acts 17:27-28
"...He is not far from each of us; for in Him we live and move and have our being, as even some of your own poets have said, 'For we also are His offspring.'"

66 Romans 5:5
"And hope does not disappoint, because the love of God has been poured out within our hearts through the Holy Spirit who was given to us."

67 Romans 8:11
"But if the Spirit of Him who raised Jesus from the dead dwells in you, He who raised Christ Jesus from

the dead will also give life to your mortal bodies through His spirit who indwells you."

68 Romans 8:16-18
"The Spirit Himself bears witness with our spirit that we are children of God, and if children, heirs also, heirs of God, and fellow heirs with Christ, if indeed we suffer with Him in order that we may also be glorified with Him.
For I consider that the sufferings of this present time are not worthy to be compared with the glory that is to be revealed to us."

69 Romans 8:24-26
"For in hope we have been saved, but hope that is seen is not hope; for why does one also hope for what he sees?

But if we hope for what we do not see, with perseverance we wait eagerly for it.
And in the same way the spirit also helps our weakness; for we do not know how to pray as we should, but the Spirit Himself intercedes for us with groanings too deep for words."

70 Romans 8:28
And we know that God causes all things to work together for good to those who love God, to those who are called according to His purpose.

71 Romans 8:38-39
"For I am convinced that neither death, nor life, nor angels, nor principalities, nor things present, nor things to come, nor powers, nor height, nor depth, nor any other created thing, shall be able to separate us from the love of God, which is in Christ Jesus our Lord."

72 Romans 15:13
"Now may the God of hope fill you with all joy and peace in believing, that you may abound in hope by the power of the Holy Spirit."

73 1 Corinthians 2:5
"...your faith should not rest on the wisdom of men, but on the power of God."

74 1 Corinthians 2:9
"But just as it is written,
Things which eye has not seen and ear has not heard,
And which have not entered the heart of man,
All that God has prepared for those who love Him."

75 1 Corinthians 6:19-20
"Or do you not know that your body is a temple of the Holy Spirit who is in you, whom you have from God, and that you are not your own?
For you have been bought with a price: therefore glorify God in your body."

76 1 Corinthians 13:12-13
   "For we now see in a mirror dimly, but then face to face; now I know in part, but then I shall know fully just as I also have been fully known.
   But now abide faith, hope, love, these three; but the greatest of these is love."

77 1 Corinthians 15:3-8
   "For I (Paul) delivered to you as of first importance what I also received, that Christ died for our sins according to the Scriptures, and that He was buried, and that He was raised on the third day according to the scriptures and that He appeared to Cephas, then to the twelve. After that He appeared to more than five hundred brethren at one time, most of whom remain until now, but some have fallen asleep; then he appeared to James, then to all the apostles; and last of all, as it were to one untimely born, He appeared to me also."

78 1 Corinthians 15:20-26, 35-38, 40, 42-47, 51-55, 57-58
   "The Order of Resurrection
   But now Christ has been raised from the dead, the first fruits of those who are asleep.
   For since by a man came death, by a man also came the resurrection of the dead.
   For as in Adam all die, so also in Christ all shall be made alive.
   But each in his own order:
   Christ the first fruits, after that those who are Christ's at His coming,

then comes the end, when He delivers up the kingdom to the God and Father, when He has abolished all rule and all authority and power.
For He must reign until He has put all His enemies under His feet.
The last enemy that will be abolished is death."
"But someone will say, "How are the dead raised? And with what kind of body do they come?" You fool! That which you sow does not come to life unless it dies; and that which you sow, you do not sow the body which is to be, but a bare grain, perhaps of wheat or of something else.
But God gives it a body just as He wished, and to each of the seeds a body of its own."
"There are also heavenly bodies and earthly bodies, but the glory of the heavenly is one, and the glory of the earthly is another."
"So also is the resurrection of the dead. It is sown a perishable body, it is raised an imperishable body; it is sown in dishonor, it is raised in glory; it is sown in weakness, it is raised in power; it is sown a natural body, it is raised a spiritual body.
If there is a natural body, there is also a spiritual body. So also it is written, "The first man, Adam, became a living soul." The last Adam became a life-giving spirit. However, the spiritual is not first, but the natural; then the spiritual.
The first man is from the earth, earthly; the second man is from heaven."
"Behold, I tell you a mystery; we shall not all sleep, but we shall all be changed, in a moment, in the twinkling

of an eye, at the last trumpet; for the trumpet will sound, and the dead will be raised imperishable, and we shall be changed. For this perishable must put on the imperishable, and this mortal must put on immortality. But when this perishable will have put on the imperishable, and this mortal will have put on immortality, then will come about the saying that is written, 'Death is swallowed up in victory. O death, where is your victory? O death, where is your sting?'"
"But thanks be to God, who gives us the victory through our Lord Jesus Christ.
Therefore, my beloved brethren, be steadfast, immovable, always abounding in the work of the Lord, knowing that your toil is not in vain in the Lord."

79 2 Corinthians 1:3-5

"Blessed be the God and Father of our Lord Jesus Christ, the Father of mercies and God of all comfort; who comforts us in all our affliction so that we may be able to comfort those who are in any affliction with the comfort with which we ourselves are comforted by God. For just as the sufferings of Christ are ours in abundance, so also our comfort is abundant through Christ."

80 2 Corinthians 4: 18

"While we look not at the things which are seen, but at the things which are not seen; for the things which are seen are temporal, but the things which are not seen are eternal."

81 2 Corinthians 5: 1
"For we know that if the earthly tent which is our house is torn down, we have a building from God. A house not made with hands, eternal in the heavens."

82 2 Corinthians 5: 6-8
"Therefore, being always of good courage, and knowing that while we are at home in the body, we are absent from the Lord—for we walk by faith, not by sight—we are of good courage, I say, and prefer rather to be absent from the body and to be at home with the Lord."

83 Ephesians 1: 5-6
"He predestined us to adoption as sons through Jesus Christ to Himself, according to the kind intention of His will, to the praise of the glory of His grace, which He freely bestowed on us in the Beloved."

84 Ephesians 3: 16-19
"He would grant you, according to the riches of His glory, to be strengthened with power through His Spirit in the inner man; so that Christ may dwell in your hearts through faith; and that you, being rooted and grounded in love, may be able to comprehend with all the saints what is the breadth and length and height and depth, and to know the love of Christ which surpasses knowledge, that you may be filled up to all the fulness of God."

85 Philippians 4: 4-7
"Rejoice in the Lord always; again I will say, rejoice! Let your forbearing spirit be known to all men. The Lord is near.
Be anxious for nothing, but in everything by prayer and supplication with thanksgiving let your requests be made known to God.
And the peace of God, which surpasses all comprehension, shall guard your hearts and your minds in Christ Jesus."

86 Colossians 2: 2-3
"...All the wealth comes from the full assurance of understanding, resulting in a true knowledge of God's mystery, that is Christ Himself, in whom are hidden all the treasures of wisdom and knowledge."

87 1 Thessalonians 4: 13-14
"But we do not want you to be uninformed, brethren, about those who are asleep, that you may not grieve, as do the rest who have no hope.
For if we believe that Jesus died and rose again, even so God will bring with Him those who have fallen asleep in Jesus."

88 1 Thessalonians 4: 16-18
"For the Lord Himself will descend from heaven with a shout, with the voice of the archangel, and with the trumpet of God; and the dead in Christ shall rise first.

Then we who are alive and remain shall be caught up together with them in the clouds to meet the Lord in the air, and thus we shall always be with the Lord. Therefore comfort each other with these words."

89 Titus 3: 7
"... being justified by His grace we might be made heirs according to the hope of eternal life."

90 Hebrews 6: 19-20
"This hope we have as an anchor of the soul, a hope both sure and steadfast and one which enters within the veil, where Jesus has entered as a forerunner for us, having become a high priest forever..."

91 Hebrews 10: 23
"Let us hold fast the confession of our hope without wavering, for He who promised is faithful."

92 Hebrews 11: 1
"Now faith is the assurance of things hoped for, the conviction of things not seen."

93 James 4: 8
"Draw near to God and He will draw near to you..."

94 1 Peter 1: 3-6
"Blessed be the God and Father of our Lord Jesus Christ, who according to His great mercy has caused us to be born again to a living hope through the resurrection of Jesus Christ from the dead, to obtain an

inheritance which is imperishable and undefiled and will not fade away, reserved in heaven for you, who are protected by the power of God through faith for a salvation ready to be revealed in the last time.
In this you greatly rejoice…"

95 1 Peter 1: 8-9
"And though you have not seen Him, you love Him, and though you do not see Him now, but believe in Him, you greatly rejoice with joy, inexpressible and full of glory, obtaining as the outcome of your faith the salvation of your souls."

96 1 John 1: 5
"…God is light, and in Him there is no darkness at all."

97 1 John 4: 16, 19
"…God is love, and the one who abides in love, abides in God, and God abides in him.
We love, because He first loved us."

98 1 John 5: 12-13
"He who has the Son has the life…These things I have written to you who believe in the name of the Son of God, in order that you may know that you have eternal life."

99 Revelation 3: 20
Behold, I stand at the door and knock: if anyone hears My voice and opens the door, I will come in to him, and will dine with him, and he with Me.

100   Revelation 21:3-5; regarding the new heaven and earth: "Behold, the tabernacle of God is among men, and He shall dwell among them, and they shall be His people, and God Himself shall be among them, and He shall wipe away every tear from their eyes; and there shall no longer be any death; there shall no longer be any mourning, or crying, or pain; the first things have passed away.

And He who sits on the throne said, 'Behold, I am making all things new.' And He said, 'Write, for these words are faithful and true.'"

Children/His Children
17, 45, 68, 83, 89

Comfort, Care, Compassion
1, 5, 7, 10, 12, 16, 24, 28, 30, 32, 35, 36, 38, 56, 58, 79, 88, 100

Counselor/Guidance
14, 15, 20

Eternal Life, Eternity
46, 47, 48, 49, 53, 54, 55, 57, 58, 62, 81, 88, 89, 94, 98

Faith
27, 38, 46, 47, 55, 56, 59, 63, 73, 77, 82, 84, 86, 92, 95, 98, 99

Heaven
41, 68, 74, 80, 88, 94, 100

Hope
6, 8, 12, 24, 31, 32, 57, 58, 60, 66, 69, 70, 72, 74, 87, 89, 90, 91, 92, 94, 100

Joy
23, 30, 34, 60, 68, 72, 85, 94, 95

Life
20, 22, 44, 48, 55, 56, 57, 59, 63, 67, 98

Light
2, 21, 40, 44, 50, 96

Love
11, 17, 28, 29, 32, 34, 46, 53, 56, 66, 71, 75, 76, 84, 95, 97

Nearness/His Presence
7, 8, 11, 14, 18, 28, 38, 52, 65, 67, 69, 75, 85, 93, 99

Peace
40, 61, 72, 85

Resurrection
37, 39, 42, 43, 53, 55, 56, 64, 67, 77, 78, 88, 94

Salvation
23, 77, 94, 95

Strength/Refuge
1, 3, 4, 5, 6, 9, 12, 13, 15, 16, 23, 25, 26, 27, 33, 34, 72, 73, 84

Sorow/Suffering
30, 56, 60, 68, 100

Trust/Truth/Waiting
4, 6, 10, 12, 13, 19, 23, 25, 26, 32, 51, 59, 62, 85

HUGS FROM HEAVEN

Hope of the Rising SON

MYSTERIOUS MOMENTS
MIRACLES TO ME

I know you can sometimes make up reasons why strange things happen; however, I believe my perception is closely in tune with reality. I do believe in the supernatural because I know it to be true. I believe in God because I have a personal relationship with Him. I believe in Jesus Christ, His Son, and the Holy Spirit, who dwells within me. Day to day, there are so many coincidences from God that I call them "God-incidences." Life is an adventure with God. It is also more calm, peaceful, and worry free.

"...I came that they may life and have it abundantly." — John 10:10

The Bible says to focus on what we can't see because it is eternal. Focus less on what you can see, because it is temporary.

"While we look not at the things which are seen, but at the things which are not seen; For the things which are seen are temporal, but the things which are not seen are eternal." — 2 Cor. 4:18

These occurrences happened during the first year or two after Brian died.

A Visitor from Heaven

The first year, as I was exceedingly distraught, I found this little miraculous sign to be consoling. As I sat in my cozy club chair, looking out my second-floor bedroom window, I saw this sight time and time again: a particular tree with a dead branch by the edge of the woods about fifteen yards away. It was thirty feet higher than the ground, which brought it about eye level with my view. Each day, as I gazed out that window for a few minutes, a red cardinal came and perched on that dead branch; so often... so often... and continued for a couple of months, maybe more (the concept of time is lost when you're grieving.) It was remarkable to me because of a legend I had heard: when a cardinal is in your yard, it is a visitor from heaven. I do believe this may be true after all. Anyway, it was comforting and reassuring. Right after Brian died, I had told him I would watch for signs of him everywhere. Between sobs, in a loving but broken voice I said: "See you around." I do not know who the visitor was, but I believe it was a visitor from heaven.

A Runner

One day, I was walking along the beach. I could hear a runner coming up behind me, rhythmic footsteps thudding on the hard, wet sand. As the sound grew closer to my right side, I moved over a little to let them by, but when I turned around to look, there was no one there.

Later, when I told my friend about this, she said, "Maybe it was Brian and he caught up with you."

The Voice of God

Another time, I was sitting on a lounge chair in our back yard. I'll never forget this: I must have dozed off when, all of a sudden, I heard a loud voice. I mean this was a powerful, LOUD SPEAKER "surround sound" voice taking up all the air space in my back yard! I was definitely awake now. I had never heard such a booming voice as this AND it was speaking casually, not yelling or angry. My ears caught what sounded like "Eth–a – ny." That's it. What in the world was that?! Ever since, I've wondered if it was "Bethany" or "Epiphany." I do not know, but it sounded to me as though there was a slight tear in an invisible curtain to another realm, and I heard a tiny part of a conversation.

Heavenly Static?

I visit Brian's grave nearly every day. As I approached his gravesite one day, I drove over a speed bump, and all of a sudden, the radio came on. It was very staticky. I did not have the radio on. I never listen to the radio. It lasted a few seconds and then it stopped. Was this another "tear in the curtain?"

"Jesus answered, 'My kingdom is not of this world…'" — John 18:36

A Marvelous Miracle

I finished babysitting my granddaughters and was on the hour drive back home. It was dark out. My overwhelming sorrow found me sobbing the whole way. What happened the next day, I believe, was the Lord's amazing way of comforting me, showing me how much He cares. I started on my morning "God Walk" along the beach. The tide was close to the shore. I looked down and there was a beautiful, fresh carnation. Its stem was wrapped in seaweed. I picked it up. It was a little wet with some sand on it. I thought, *Oh, wow, this is so pretty. How unusual to find such an item along the shoreline.* I had further to go, so I thought, *I'll just leave this here for someone else to find. If it's still here when I return in a couple miles, I'll take it. Thank you, God.* I continued to walk, but about forty steps later, I saw another one! It was fresh and wrapped in seaweed just like the other one! I picked it up. I thought how really strange this was; but as I walked, I found another one, the same distance apart. It got stranger and stranger because it happened again and again and again and again… Every time, the carnation was a bit sandy, but fresh and beautiful, wrapped carefully in seaweed, the same way. As I went along, every time I picked up a flower, God seemed to be telling me: "I love you." When I returned the way I came, the first carnation was still there. God had told me "I love you" more than 20 times! I had collected a bouquet of love from GOD! When I got home, I put my flowers in a vase with water. The wet sand had dried and fell off. How beautiful was my bouquet! I will never forget this experience and the way God cared for me. Thank you for loving me.

Sandy Bouquet of Love

Bouquet of Love, at Home

Singing Cardinal

A couple years later, as I was walking toward Brian's gravestone, I made a wish: *I wish a cardinal would fly over and sit on your stone, right now.* And just then, a cardinal DID fly near and perch on a branch right next to the stone. My mouth opened in amazement. He sang a few songs, then flew away, my mouth still wide open. I had never seen a cardinal around there and I haven't seen one since. I would not mind seeing another one, though.

Thank you, God.

Conclusion

I want to share my hope with you, that you may know it, too.

I have learned and grown since ten years have passed.

When my son died, I was ready to burst with emotion. Feeling as though I broke in half, writing to him released the feelings of pain. Those feelings are now in the depths of my ocean heart, because I've learned to live on the surface. In the beginning, the shock wave is in front of your face. You can't see anything else. Gradually, over time, the shock and pain subside so that, instead of crying every hour of every day, you cry once a day, then once a week. This is good grief and necessary. Go through it. Do not avoid it. You will start to have better days, then good days. It all depends on what you choose to think about. Dwelling on regrets will not heal you. Decide that when you have pondered them enough, then let them go. There is no point in feeling the same pain over and over again for the rest of your life. Go forth with a positive outlook. I'm not saying that a good outlook will free you from pain; I'm saying that it will allow you to heal, and eventually feel much better. This is where Christian hope comes in. Balance it with your sorrow, and joy will also live in your heart. Keeping your faith is of utmost importance. You have HOPE; the hope of seeing your loved one again, and the hope of Heaven.

Keep reading your Bible, because it is actually alive with God's love for you and His words for you. He speaks to you through it! You must "seek in order to find." Where is God in all of this?

> You have HOPE; the hope of seeing your loved one again, and the hope of Heaven.

"'For I know the plans that I have for you', declares the Lord, 'plans for welfare and not for calamity to give you a future and a hope. Then you will call upon Me and come and pray to Me, and I will listen to you. And you will seek Me and find Me, when you search for Me with all your heart. And I will be found by you', declares the Lord..." — Jer. 29:11-14

Every moment you spend with your loved ones is precious. See them through the eyes of God, and you will *see*. Listen to them carefully. Look them in the eyes. Let them know you are letting God's light shine through you to them. How would it be if you could have just one more moment with your loved one who died? Even just one minute!

Express, release, cry, weep, sob—heal. Heal so you can function without walking around like you're a robot. Live and grow closer to God. He is the ultimate *comforter*.

"...In Thy presence is fullness of joy." — Ps. 16:11

The Lord is near. Your loved one is with Him. He is also near you. He lives in your heart: you carry Him everywhere.

What are you to gain by reading my letters to Brian? Compassion from a soul who understands the anguish of your pain: souls are connected by God.

"...Pour out your heart before Him. God is a refuge for us." — Ps. 62:8

"He who dwells in the shelter of the Most High will abide in the shadow of the Almighty." — Ps. 91:1

The Hope of Heaven

The next place we go is heaven. Our lives on earth are only the beginning. Heaven is where we become the epitome of the essence of who we are. The battle has already been won. Jesus died for us. Through His blood we are saved. Only believe.

"...in Me you may have peace. In the world you have tribulation, but take courage; I have overcome the world." — John 16:33

"Therefore you too now have sorrow; but I will see you again, and your heart will rejoice, and no one takes your joy away from you.". — John 16: 22

Remember His amazing gift of LOVE and FORGIVENESS: He loves you and cares for you. Trust in His guidance.

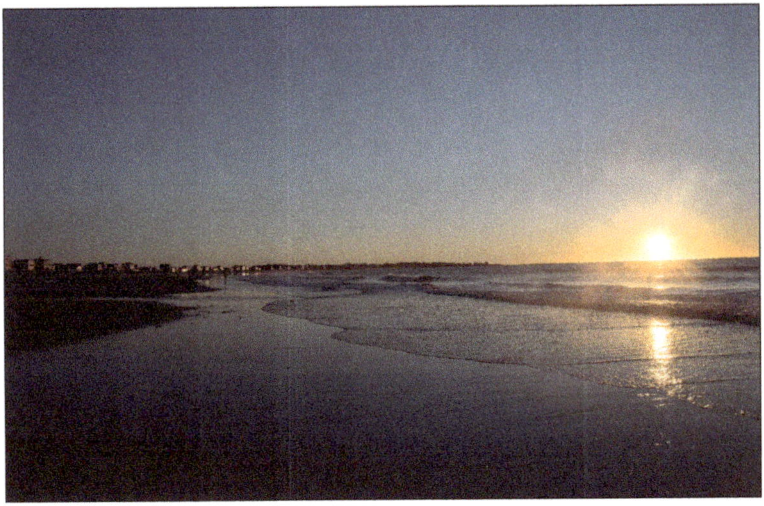